LIVING PLACES

Other books in this series:

Made with Oak
Good Lives
Rooms with a View
Around the House

LIVING PLACES

by Herbert H. Wise
and Jeffrey Weiss

New York
London
Tokyo

International Standard Book Number: 0-8256-3067-3
Library of Congress Catalog Card Number: 76-8071
Printed in Japan

In Great Britain: Book Sales Ltd., 78 Newman Street, London W1P 3LA.
In Canada: Gage Trade Publishing, P.O. Box 5000, 164 Commander Blvd.,
          Agincourt, Ontario M1S 3C7.
In Japan: Quick Fox, 4-26-22 Jingumae, Shibuya-ku, Tokyo 150.
In Germany: Music Sales Gmbh, Kölner Strasse 199, D-5000 Cologne 90
          West Germany.

Book and cover design: Christine Yorke
Production: Richard Spector
Lighting and photo assistance: David Frazier

LIVING PLACES

Living Places is our attempt to show how diverse people from
across the country have chosen to renovate or remodel their
homes to reflect and enhance their lives. Some have conceived of
and executed the work themselves. Some have had access to the
best architects and contractors. All of the results have imagination.
While we give some practical advice in the section at the back of
the book, we do not offer this as a technical how-to-do-it guide.
Rather, we believe that by visiting the homes of people of taste
and style, you will, by breathing in their various interpretations,
be able to translate them into your own conceptions, which can
be applied to your own homes.

Good taste is an elusive term to define. That's why we've tried to
demonstrate what resourceful and intelligent people (who have
often had access to substantial amounts of money) can do when
they decide to bend an existing space to meet their vision of where
they want to live their daily lives. We feel that whether it's the
meticulous but inexpensive do-it-yourself job of a Berkeley builder
and his wife or the elaborate and obviously costly renovation of an
old warehouse into a town house with a walled outdoor pool,
there's something to be learned and applied to your own living
space.

What are the things that are important to you? Have you things to display? Are they important in themselves—valuable art, for example—or because of their charm and your love of them—such as wall hangings and decorations that are pastel imitations of original tapestries? Do you want your bathroom to be an efficient machine, or is it a place of fantasy and splendor in hand-painted tile? Is your kitchen a place to bring food from, or is it the focal point in the home, a place where the family gathers? The answers to these questions, and many others—who comes to visit? is life formal or informal? are there children?—are all crucial factors in determining what designs and decorations are right for you.

We traveled to San Francisco, Berkeley, Mill Valley, and Sausalito; to many communities, including Walnut Creek and Topanga in the Los Angeles area; to the Garden District, Uptown, and the French Quarter in New Orleans; to Capitol Hill in Washington, D.C.; to Greenwich, Connecticut, to Cambridge, Massachusetts; and we toured the many different neighborhoods of Manhattan—SoHo, the Village, and the Upper East Side— to discover just how people have fashioned their living places to suit their practical needs and their dreams. Naturally, a house structured around a solar-heated organically composted bathroom designed to grow orchids is more suitable to the climate of Sausalito than Cambridge. So do bear in mind that many of the design solutions that follow are regional solutions. The trick is to *adapt these concepts to your own needs.*

In the pages that follow the photographs you'll find basic hints that should help you to begin to plan your renovation. Included are rough guidelines for the price and scope of kitchen and bathroom remodeling (the most frequently contemplated work), advice on choosing a contractor and an architect if you wish to engage them, and advice on how to finance your work. But it's the photographs more than anything we can write that will show the way.

In finding the living places shown here, we met many wonderful people—friends we hope to keep. We had help from Ann Dowie, Carole Baxter, Gloria Amedee, Sarah Simon, Al Jaffe, Mark Goldschmidt, Sybil Joseph, Kathleen Fliegal, Claudia Coonrad, and Suzanne Opton in finding places to photograph. To everyone—thanks.

—Herbert Wise,
Jeffrey Friedman-Weiss
August 1976

SOME PRACTICAL ADVICE

Like so many things in life, renovation and remodeling are intimately connected with money. Determining the cost of changing your home will be your first step in deciding what is going to be done. Most people find that doubling both the amount of money and time you figure you are going to spend doing the job is not an overly cautious rule of thumb. In an attempt to help you to get a fix on what's involved, we're going to lay out some ground rules. However, because the cost of labor and materials is always going up and because the special aspects of your own plan may make it impossible to apply conventional estimating techniques, we stress careful planning and thinking.

There are two broad categories of renovation: structural and cosmetic. Of course, the two are often intertwined. Building an extra bathroom or moving a kitchen constitute the two most common kinds of structural renovation; similarly, replacing kitchen cabinets or retiling a bathroom floor are frequent cosmetic renovations. Additional electrical outlets (and hence circuitry) will frequently be necessary additions, ones often over-looked until the invoice arrives.

WHERE TO BEGIN

Most construction and renovation jobs require that you deal with a contractor. He is the instrument through which your ideas and plans will be transformed into reality. However, selecting one can be tricky, and is worth agonizing over. Most general contractors are independent entrepreneurs who go in and out of business faster than used-car salesmen. A routine check of a contractor's previous customers and a call to the local Better Business Bureau may help you avoid the real sharks.

Hiring a contractor is like voting for President, except worse. Both will make promises, pronouncements and prognostications; both will talk about rising costs and shrinking pay checks. However, when the President doesn't honor his campaign pledges, his platform will not literally collapse under him. Yours might. Therefore, the safest way to hire a contractor short of divine inspiration is to know what you want and to have a clear idea of what you have to spend. This means extensive planning.

Most problems with contractors arise because of communication failures. Construction is a highly technical field with a precise vocabulary and nomenclature. The layman often finds he simply cannot talk intelligently with a contractor, and vice versa, because there are two different languages involved. And so there are translators—architects. Even if you know exactly what you want, and expect to do the work yourself, an architect can be a valuable asset, one worth investing money in. A good architect will be able to reveal the full potential of your home by suggesting the best ways it can be made to work for you and your family. A consultation fee paid for an architect's advice before you formulate final plans could, in the long run, save a great deal of money, as it well might help you avoid disastrous mistakes or simply find cheaper and more efficient solutions to your particular problems.

Once having decided how you are going to proceed, the next step will be to make your plan and specification list. An architect will do this for you. If you are going to plan and manage the job yourself, your best bet is to buy *Architectural Graphic Standards*. This book supplies the standard dimensions of sinks, cabinets, lavatories, dishwashers, etc.; includes detailed instructions for laying out a room grid, which will show the existing electrical, plumbing, and structural aspects of the room; and even includes cut-outs of furniture to mock up a complete room. When you are sure you know exactly what you want, then decide whether you will hire a general contractor and relax (so to speak), or act as your own main contractor, dealing separately with and supervising workmen of different trades. Of course, the more money you have, the more options you'll have.

HOW TO FIND AN ARCHITECT

Architects are not allowed to advertise or solicit, and so must rely upon their work and word of mouth as the best source of referral. Seeing something you like may be the most important test, particularly if you are only relying on the architect for design and not for construction supervision. Approaching an architect with details of your project will not commit you in any way. You are free to consult as many architects as you wish before making up your mind which of them you want. Most architects will be happy to give you "partial service," which is preliminary advice at the planning stage or a recommendation on the best way to achieve your object. The more prestigious architects will have a standard fee per hour for such consultation; however, those who are less well established will usually agree to bargain with you. This hourly rate will normally be used as the basis for calculating the fee for the next two stages of the architect's work—the designing and the calculating of probable cost. The fee for *full* architectural service on an existing building will be based on a percentage of the total job—contractors, materials, labor, and so on.

HOW TO FIND A CONTRACTOR

Finding a good contractor is quite difficult, as the inexperienced customer will frequently be substantially victimized by his own ignorance and inexperience. The safest way is to rely on a recommendation. But to safeguard all parties, no contractor should be asked to give an estimate for a job without being shown written specifications for the work involved. The moment you give a contractor leeway to choose a size or height or detail, or to vary from the plan without quoting a new cost, is the moment trouble starts. His choice may not be yours, and what seems to you to be a ten-minute adjustment may be to him a substantial structural alteration.

HOW MUCH WILL IT COST?

Before the days of double-digit inflation, a good guideline for estimating how much a given renovation would cost would be to add 60 percent for labor to the cost of materials. But since the price of everything has become so fluid, use that principle only as the roughest guide. As this is written in the summer of 1976, the cost of remodeling a bathroom in New York City—retiling, plastering, and connecting new fixtures to existing plumbing—ranges from a minimum of $2,000, to a middle range of $4,000 for better but nonetheless standard fixtures and tile, to more than twice that for hand-glazed or imported tile or any custom plumbing such as steam or sauna connections. Local contractors will quote prices on standard kitchen renovations in terms of the cost for tiling, and the cost of new appliances. Be advised that such prices do not take into account any electrical or plumbing work and refer to "standard" quality and size materials. Any deviation from standard often results in very large increased costs. Again, as a rough rule of thumb, and assuming your old appliances will be reconnected in place to existing electric, plumbing, and gas service, one can estimate that a modest kitchen renovation will cost no less than $3,500. If you desire the custom personal appearance of many of the kitchens in this book, the cost will be very much greater. Often you can save considerable amounts of money by doing the unskilled parts of the job yourself. Ripping out old counters, for example, requires only muscle. Replacing them is the skilled work. Contractors are frequently eager to have the dirtier parts of the job done by you. You'll find that very often local craftspeople and artisans will be skilled builders and carpenters, and will offer their artistic talents for laborer's wages. Using this kind of help may entail special frustrations and risks, but people of integrity and ability will often produce brilliant interpretations of what you require. Since they regard renovation work as a sideline to their real vocations as artists—and expect to be treated accordingly—they often work inexpensively.

A wide variety of home-improvement loans is available these days. Banks seem to be actively competing with one another for this kind of business, so it's wise to shop as carefully for your financing as for your labor and materials. Local credit unions sometimes offer planning advice and guidance to reputable workers. As in all other aspects of renovation and remodeling, be cautious.

We hope the sober tone we've taken in this section hasn't been too off-putting. The spell of the homes in the photographs is perhaps the best antidote. We've found there is wonderful pleasure in fashioning your own living space, even if it's often fraught with anxiety and expense.

ACKNOWLEDGMENTS

We wish to thank the many home owners, architects, contractors, and designers who graciously allowed us to photograph their homes and their work. Many preferred to remain anonymous, therefore this listing only partially reflects the many homes we photographed.

In Berkeley: the Cohens, Rick and Marlene Millikan.

In Cambridge: Crissman and Solomon, Mrs. William LeMessier, Mr. and Mrs. David Rockefeller, Jr., Mr. and Mrs. William Truslow, Mr. and Mrs. Donald Tucker.

In Los Angeles: Tom Braverman, Raymond Kappe, Edward Killingsworth, Michael Leventhal and Howard Rosen, H.B. Leydenstrot, Mrs. Judson Morgan, Michael Shotwell.

In Mill Valley: Bill Kirsch, Ivan Poutiatine.

In New York: Richard Hamner, Neil and Chris Marshad, Rick Meyerwitz, Mr. and Mrs. Alexander Milliken, Boyd Morrow.

In San Francisco: John Field, Karen and Butch Kardum, Herbert McLaughlin, Charles Rushing, Ken Schubert.

In Sausalito: Jacques Ullman.